R U M I
Thief of Sleep

شمس تبریزی بیا کز لطف خود
شوق ها در عاشقان افکنده ای

Shams-e Tabrizi biyaa, kaz lotf-e khod
Shoghhaa dar aasheghaan afkande'i

sham of / tabriz / come/appear / because of /
    kindness/grace of / yours
enthusiasm/passion / in the / lover / you have evoked

*A*ppear O Shams-e Tabriz, your boundless grace
Has enraptured the lovers on the path.

R U M I
Thief of Sleep

Quatrains from the Persian
Translations by
Shahram Shiva

Foreword by
Deepak Chopra

HOHM PRESS
Prescott, Arizona

Cover design: Kim Johansen
Page design and layout: J. Pratt, Alpha-Cat Design

Library of Congress Cataloging-in-Publication Data
Jalal al-Din Rumi, Maulana, 1207-1273
 [Divan-i Shams-i Tabrizi. English. Selections]
 Rumi, thief of sleep: quatrains from the Persian/translations
by Shahram Shiva; foreward by Deepak Chopra.
  p. cm.
 ISBN 1-890772-05-4 (alk. paper)
  I. Shiva, Shahram. II. Title.

PK6481.D6 E5 2000
891'.5511-dc21

00-04093

The quatrains in this book were originally published in
Rending the Veil: Literal and Poetic Translations of Rumi,
by Shahram Shiva; Hohm Press, 1995,
ISBN: 0-934252-46-7

07 06 05 04 03 02 01   6 5 4 3 2

HOHM PRESS
P.O. Box 2501
Prescott, AZ 86302
800-381-2700
Printed in the U.S.A. on recycled paper using soy ink.
www.hohmpress.com
Shahram Shiva's web site: www.rumi.net

To the little known Persian
aspect of Lord Shiva.

CONTENTS

FOREWORD

by *Deepak Chopra*
author of *How to Know God*

T.S. Eliot once said that poetry is a raid on the inarticulate. The words of Moulana Jalaluddin Rumi have been helping me to dive into the unfathomable abyss of spirit ever since I was six years old. My father would take me to *Moushaira*—evening concerts where great poets would recite not only their own work but also the poems of Hafiz, Kabir, Rumi, Ghalib and others. The words were in Farsi, which my father spoke, so as I sat next to him or sometimes on his lap, he would explain them to me in English or Hindi. No matter—even when I didn't understand, I experienced the shift in consciousness that was occurring around me and I felt a part of it. I experienced *exultation of spirit.*

Today as a medical doctor I realize that words can heal, that they can make us feel safe, that they can transform our lives and bring joy, meaning, and purpose in our lives. Words can bring us closer to God. Such are the words of Rumi. In *Thief of Sleep*, Shahram Shiva (who embodies the culture, the wisdom and the history of Sufism in his very genes) brings us the healing experience. I recommend his book to anyone who wishes *to remember*. The Sufi word for remembrance is *Zikir*. *Zikir* is the remembrance of divinity within and around us. We do not need to struggle or learn to become experts. We simply need to remember. *RUMI: Thief of Sleep* will help you do that.

INTRODUCTION

The "Thief of Sleep"
Is wishing my altar wet with tears.
Without a sound,
not even a breath,
in total stillness,
he grabbed me in dream,
threw me in water,
in sweet water.
Now the rose and the thorn are one.
And the fragrance,
is rejuvenating Paradise.

*I*n Persian, there are four levels of friendship each relating to a degree in closeness and intimacy: *Aashenaa* (to know someone casually), *Doost* (a close friend), *Rafeegh* (your best friend) and *Yaar* (your inseparable lover). However, these levels are independent of the type of physical connection you have with someone. These degrees of closeness explain your deep soul connection with another being; your spouse, therefore, may only be your *Aashenaa*, or you may have a perfect platonic relationship with a *Yaar*. Some mystics measure their intimacy with God and the Beloved by using these levels. For Rumi, the Beloved and Shams were one, and both (as one) were his *Yaar*. That could explain why Rumi's verses are being dubbed "love poems." Should they be anything less? Rumi is a mystic of the highest order who reached a rare level of divine intimacy with the Beloved. Each one of Rumi's poems, spoken in the moment, is an autobiographical account of the transformation of his being. Every time a Rumi poem is recited that experience is lived again.

If there is one constant in the universe it is love—the core thread connecting all of creation. It is said the Earth orbits around the Sun because of love. The Shiva/Shakti (beloved/lover, creator/creation) principal in Hinduism is an accurate, romantic and poetic explanation of the process of creation. Why is there a creation after all? Why does the creator in its limitless insight continue to be the observer of what the mystics call a "carnival" or "theater"? The only acceptable explanation is love. It is only when you love someone in the truest form that you will not tire of being with them or watching them grow. This universe is an expression of a pure, focused, ever-replenishing Love-Energy. Is it any wonder that Rumi's popularity is growing so widely?

We belong to a creation hooked on love, obsessed with love and all its trappings. We languish in its absence and feel betrayed by its counterfeits. We fantasize about it, build castles in the clouds for it. Some of the world's best cliched references are about everlasting love. The most watched movie on the planet recently wasn't an action-adventure (although it had plenty of it), nor was it about giant animals roaming the earth millions of years ago, nor was it a science-fiction set in a galaxy far, far away with a plot based on Eastern mythology. It was a simple story of young love served with a full entrée of obstacles (on fine china) and alas not a happy ending in sight.

Every moment of every day we see and hear around us expressions of love, in its varied forms. Through all media, in nature, even in sub-atomic particles. Physicists hypothesize about minute particles of opposing polarity uniting for a nano-moment just in time to burn up and disappear together. Have you heard of a more romantic tale? The most effective and damaging computer virus to date came with the message "I Love You." The users worldwide couldn't help but open a file with such an inviting title. Every atom of every particle can't help but project the essence of its constitution. For a universe hooked on Love, how fortunate we are to call Rumi its emissary.

To explore the phenomenon of Rumi's popularity further, I recently asked a group of about fifty participants in one of my poetry workshops to explain why Rumi meant so much to them. I then grouped their responses into twelve distinct categories: 1) Non-Intellectual: They found Rumi to cater to their hearts, emotions and instincts rather than intellects. 2) Levels: They found many levels in Rumi's poetry. The more they learned about Rumi, the more they appreciated his depth and were encouraged to dig deeper. 3) Unity: They found the sense of unity and universal siblinghood in Rumi's poetry to be very attractive. 4) Friend: They found him to be as a friend. 5) Personal: Reading Rumi for them is a very personal and intimate experience. They associate themselves with him. 6) Grace Descending: Every time a Rumi poem is recited they feel Grace descending. 7) Longing: They associated with the sense of longing in Rumi's poems. 8) Love Affair: Rumi is like a lover to some of the participants. 9) Religious Bridge: They found Rumi to form a religious bridge for the Moslems in this country. Through Rumi some Moslems found a wider acceptance in the U.S. 10) They Don't Even Like Poetry: Some expressed that they don't even like poetry, but they love reading Rumi poems. 11) Participate in the Process: They found Rumi extremely expressive and found themselves participating in Rumi's own process. 12) Guide: They found Rumi to be a spiritual guide for them.

Hindu mystics refer to it as *turya,* in science it is known as the "hypnagogic state" and Rumi calls it the *Thief of Sleep*—yet another name for the Beloved. It is a place in between the dream and the waking state, which usually happens in the very early morning hours (around 4:00AM). In this state the body feels paralyzed, the mouth is slightly open and one may experience vivid spiritual visions that often include visitations from deities, saints and prophets. Throughout the centuries, countless revelations and teachings have been passed on to mystics in this way, and it is also a way of receiving creative inspiration. Many times have I found myself being called upon by the *Thief of Sleep,* either for a visitation or musical inspiration. Complete musical scores of various genres through numerous cultures have been "performed" in the ears of fortunate ones with perfect clarity by the *Thief of Sleep*—or should we refer to this one as the muse? May the *Thief of Sleep* grant you an inspiring visit.

In the past dozen years that I have been fortunate to be translating Rumi, one of my goals has been to bring readers closer to the majesty of the Persian of Rumi. Rumi *lives* in the Persian language. The Persian of Rumi is a miracle. The Persian of Rumi is one of the most exquisite sounds. The Persian of Rumi heals, uplifts, mesmerizes, cradles the heart, inspires growth, enlightens, kisses you on your right cheek, then on the left, warms your soul and brings you closer to yourself. The Persian of Rumi is your Yaar (lover) who wraps his or her arms around you, holds you close, and whispers precious secrets in your ear. Like a perfect lover, he or she will never abandon you; he or she will not put you down, nor will the *Yaar* leave you for another. The Persian of Rumi is here all for you.

Rumi was an extraordinary man, who led an extraordinary life and left behind a treasure chest of the finest rubies and emeralds, each as large and limitless as his heart. The poems gathered in this book are among those jewels. They are also selections from my second book, *Rending the Veil: Literal* and *Poetic Translations of Rumi*. In *Rending the Veil* I tried to bring you closer to Rumi's own voice in Persian through an easy-to-follow four-step process. *Rending The Veil* enables the reader to sound out the Persian of Rumi and see the structure and rhyme scheme of the original poems through a transliteration phase. You could then know the meaning of each word via a word-for-word translation process. Finally, it offers a poetic version of the 252 poems, very close to Persian. The Persian calligraphy of each poem is also included. In both *Rending The Veil and Thief Of Sleep,* the original reference numbers from two editions of Rumi's *Divan-e Shams-e Tabrizi* accompany each poem and are followed by AK for Amir Kabir Press and UT for University of Tehran Press. (Please see *Rending the Veil* for more information.)

Thief of Sleep is a selection of the best of the poetic versions from *Rending the Veil.* It offers translations in English that are honoring of Rumi's original voice. The aim is to present verses that are closest to Rumi's own words without sounding too literal and foreign. In a world filled with versions of his poems by poets with no knowledge of Rumi's own voice in Persian, I hope that you find this offering as a welcome change, and that the love expressed in these precious lines may bless your home and your heart.

Many hearts of gratitude to Deepak Chopra for his continuing and generous support of my work; to Regina Sara Ryan and Dasya Zuccarello of Hohm Press, and to Pamela Miles for feedback on this introduction.

May the wisdom of Shams continually inspire us and may his compassion be a guiding light on our path to unity.

To Love,
Shahram Shiva

THE QUATRAINS

The thief of my sleep
Is wishing my altar wet with my tears.
He grabbed me in silence and threw me in water
A water with a sweetness that sweetens my own.

3 AK

My jewel turns pure from the Beloved's ruby wine.
My cup starts wailing, groaning because of me.
I have been drinking cup after cup after cup of this wine
I have become the wine and the wine has become me.

9 AK

The repetition of God's name brings light to the full moon.
This repetition brings back the lost ones to the path
of truth.
Make this your word, for every morning and evening
prayer
The saying of "There is no God but Allah."

11 AK

There is a life-force within your soul, seek that life.
There is a gem in the mountain of your body, seek
that mine.
O traveler, if you are in search of That
Don't look outside, look inside yourself and seek That.

32 UT

The Beloved weaned me with praise and riches.
He tailored a sheath of veins and skin for my soul.
This body is His Robe, and I, a Sufi, reside in His heart.
All the world a Khaneghah, and He is its master.

33 AK

If you can't grasp us, to this alley do not come.
If you can't strip your clothes, to this stream do not come.
This is the center of the compass, no place for cowards
Stay on your side, to this side do not come.

60 AK

O you, alone in the sky like the Sun. Come.
Without your face the garden and the leaves are all yellow.
   Come.
Without you, the universe is dust and powder. Come.
Without you, this drunken gathering is cold. Come.

64 UT

*O*ur drunkenness does not come from drinking wine.
Our gathering, so festive, it is not from harp or rubaab.
Without the cupbearer, without a companion, without
   musicians or wine
We are dishevelled and dizzy like wasted drunkards.

82 UT

What sort of day is today, there are two suns in the sky.
Today is different from any other day.
There is a call to a wedding from the heavens,
To the people of the heart saying, "Good news, this is
    your day, today."

130 UT

The moment that I turn around you
Is the gathering of Saaqi, wine and cup.
The moment you see the magnificent shine of grace
Your soul, stunned and amazed, is like Moses son
    of Emran.

130 AK

Tonight I am spinning around the house of the Beloved.
I'll turn and turn till dawn, around His house.
Every savoring drink has been named after Him
This skull in my hands is the Beloved's cup.

171 AK

Have justice. To Love is a virtuous act
And harm is to the one who is of a harmful nature.
What you call love is only lust
Between lust and love there is a great distance.

175 AK

O my soul, there is a link between your heart and mine.
And my heart is looking for that path.
My heart is clear and pure like water
And pure water is a perfect mirror for moonlight.

185 AK

Don't speak of the night for our days have no night.
In every religion there is love, but love has no religion.
Love is an ocean, without borders and shores
Where many drown, yet groans of regret or a calling
    to God is not heard.

232 AK

They say, "Love mixed with intellect is better
In every faith, discrimination is better."
Yes, your words shine like gold, yet
My life, offered to Shams-e Tabriz, is better.

245 UT

The Beloved shuts the gate of union, and blocks my way.
The Beloved breaks my heart with pains and sorrow.
From now on, my broken heart and I will wait at the gate.
For He prefers those with a broken heart.

245 AK

Suddenly the drunken sweetheart appeared out of my door.
She drank a cup of ruby wine and sat by my side.
Seeing and holding the lockets of her hair
My face became all eyes, and my eyes all hands.

264 UT

Every day, the sweetheart appears anew
With a cup full of passion and excitement in her hands.
If I accept, the flask of intellect will crack,
If I don't, she won't let me be in peace.

265 UT

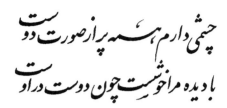

Cheshmee daaram, hameh por az soorat-e doost
Baa-deedeh ma-raa khosh ast, chon doost daroost
Az deedeh-o doost, farghkardan nah nekoost
Yaa doost bejaaye deedeh, yaa deedeh khodoost

these eyes | I have | all full | of | face of the | Beloved
with the sight | to me | pleasing | it is | because |
    the Beloved | is in it
of | the sight and | the Beloved | to differentiate | is not |
    good/fitting either | the Beloved | in the place of |
    the sight | or | the sight | is him

$\mathcal{M}$y eyes are full with the face of the Beloved.
I am happy with the sight, because I see the Beloved.
There is no difference between the sight and the Beloved.
Either the Beloved is in the sight, or the sight in the
    Beloved.

285 AK

This great thunder is coming from my Saturn.
This fragrance comes from my garden.
He is that Thing which is on my heart and soul.
Until He goes—where can He go? He is mine.

300 UT

In the path of union, the wise man and the mad man are one.
In the way of love, close friends and strangers are one.
That one who has tasted the wine of union with the
    supreme soul,
In his faith, the Ka'be and an idol temple are one.

306 AK

*I*n love, aside from sipping the wine of timelessness,
    nothing else exists.
There is no reason for living except for giving one's life.
I said, "First I know you, then I die."
He said, "For the one who knows Me, there is no dying."

311 AK

*T*his chest, so full of flames, is a lesson of His school.
And today my illness is His fever.
I'll stay away from what the doctor recommends
Except for the wine and sugar which spills from His lips.

318 UT

$\mathcal{A}$ny spot that I place my head, He is the cushion.
In all the six directions and out, He is the deity.
Garden, flower, nightingale, samaa, and a companion.
These are all an excuse. He is my only reason.

319 UT

Inside and outside, he surrounds my heart.
My body, my soul, my veins and my blood, are all Him.
How can blasphemy and faith fit into my being?
My life has no value, for He is everything.

321 UT

*T*he memory of you blinds my vision of you, O Beloved.
The glow of your face is the mask of your face, O Beloved.
The thought of your lips, deprives me of your lips
The thought of your lips, is the veil of your lips, O Beloved.

329 UT

I have become mad—how can you expect me to sleep?
How could a mad person find a way to sleep?
Because God does not sleep, He is free from it.
One who is crazy for God, also does not sleep.

336 AK

I drank that wine of which the soul is its vessel.
Its ecstasy has stolen my intellect away.
A light came and kindled a flame in the depth of my soul.
A light so radiant that the sun orbits around it like
    a butterfly.

344 AK

*A*s long as the face of that enviable angel is in my heart,
Who is happy as me in all this universe?
I swear, I only know how to live blissfully,
I hear about sorrow but I have no idea what it is.

351 UT

Both existence and nonexistence are alien to me,
Yet escaping from the two is not a noble deed.
If from the wonders I have in my heart
I don't become mad, it is because of madness itself.

366 UT

When the sweet glance of my true love caught my eyes,
Like alchemy, it transformed my copper-like soul.
I searched for Him with a thousand hands,
He stretched out His arms and clutched my feet.

411 UT

I have lost myself in God, and now God is mine.
Don't look for Him in every direction, for He is
   in my soul.
I am the Sultan. I would be lying
If I said that there is someone who is my Sultan.

422 AK

*T*he faithless heart is in grief and sorrow.
One without faith is not truly alive.
Didn't I tell you that no one would remember me
Except for sorrow. A thousand praises to that sorrow.

435 UT

$\mathcal{E}$very day my heart falls deeper in the pain of your sorrow.
Your cruel heart is weary of me already.
You have left me alone yet your sorrow stays.
Truly, your sorrow is more faithful than you are.

447 AK

It is love that brings happiness to people.
It is love that gives joy to happiness.
My mother didn't give birth to me, that love did.
A hundred blessings and praises to that love.

449 UT

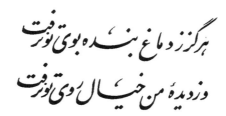

Hargez ze damaagh-e bandeh, booye to naraft
Vaz deedeye man, khiyaale rooye to naraft
Dar aarezooye to, omr bordam shab-o rooz
Omram hameh raft-o, aarezooye to naraft

never | of | nose of | mine | smell of | you | left not
and of | sight of | mine | thought of | face of | you | left
   not
in the | desire of | you | lifetime | I passed | night and |
   day
my life | all | is gone and | the desire of | you | left not

*Y*our scent has never left my nose;
The image of your face has never left my sight.
For lifetimes I have longed for you, day and night.
My life is now consumed, yet my desire for you is still
   the same.

450 AK

The lover like the sun will shine.
The lover like the atoms will turn.
When the spring breeze of love begins to swirl,
Any branch that is not dead will dance.

466 UT

I look at the Beloved, and His face turns red.
And if I don't look He causes my heart to ache.
In the pool of His face stars are visible
Without His water, my water is nothing but mud.

479 UT

Can one who has not tasted wine fall asleep?
The one who hears news of Him, how then can he sleep?
Love whispers in my ears all night.
Only grief comes to one who falls asleep without Him.

485 AK

Does life have any meaning to one who has found you?
Does wife, children, and livelihood have any meaning?
You turn people mad and then offer the two worlds.
Does the world have any meaning for one maddened by
    your love?

492 AK

My verses, love songs, and poems were taken by the water.
   The clothes that I didn't even own were taken by
      the flood.
   Good, bad, asceticism, and my Persian blood
   Moonlight gave, and again, moonlight took away.

508 UT

With the Beloved's water of life, no illness remains
In the Beloved's rose garden of union, no thorn remains.
They say there is a window from one heart to another
How can there be a window where no wall remains?

511 AK

There was a red hot glow when the twins joined together.
There was the sound of your voice in the stream
   of the heart.
Pure water is now a mirage, blazing fire cold like snow,
The legend of life is now passed—was it just a dream?

512 AK

I am blasphemy and religion, pure and unpure;
Old, young, and a small child.
If I die, don't say that he died.
Say he was dead, became alive, and was taken by the
   Beloved.

519 UT

*A*ll it took was the dew drops of love to form Adam's
   body of mud.
A few drops and a universe of seductions and sensations
   was set.
It brought down a hundred lances of love on the veins
   of the soul
One drop leaked and became what we call "the heart."

521 AK

*A*ny soul that drank the nectar of your passion was lifted.
From that water of life he is in a state of elation.
Death came, smelled me, and sensed your fragrance
   instead
From then on, death lost all hope of me.

522 AK

When I think of you my heart starts to pound.
Tears of blood drip down my face.
When news from the Friend is first heard,
My poor heart lifts up from the body toward the sky.

547 UT

This aloneness is worth more than a thousand lives.
This freedom is worth more than all the lands on earth.
To be one with the truth for just a moment,
Is worth more than the world and life itself.

550 UT

Out of your love the fire of youth will rise.
In the chest, visions of the soul will rise.
If you are going to kill me, kill me, it is all right.
When the friend kills, a new life will rise.

557 UT

Your passion is just an excuse.
Your drunkenness is just a song.
Why do you strike me with the blade of unkindness,
When only the touch of a whip is enough?

577 UT

The breath of the fortunate ones is fragrant as a rose.
And of the unfortunate it is sharp like a thorn.
Speaking of roses, the thorn will escape from the fire.
Speaking of thorns, a rose will remain in the fire.

579 UT

When your love set my heart ablaze,
All that I had turned ashes, except for your love.
Intellect, achievement, and books were placed
    on the shelves—
Poetry, love songs, and couplets were learned instead.

616 UT

I am blind to the truth, only God knows,
Why He is making me laugh in my heart.
My heart resembles a stem of a flower
Which the morning breeze gently shakes about.

646 UT

I want the particles that come from your being.
Let the sight always bathe in the dust of your feet.
I am joyous and cheerful at the Beloved's cruelty
It is the cruelty that confirms the Beloved's loyalty.

650 AK

I wish my heart to be one with sorrow.
What wonder to feel the hand of His sorrow!
Know this, O heartless heart, and behold His sorrow.
Before long, you will learn that His sorrow is indeed
    His true self.

651 AK

*O*n the path of love, if you find rest for even a moment
Then what business do you have lining up with the lovers?
Sharp and hard like a thorn, then approach the Beloved
    delicate as a rose
So you can hold Him in your arms and have Him by
    your side.

673 AK

درکوی خـرابات تکبرنخرند
مردی بـرکوی خرابات برند

آنجاچورسـے مقامری باید کرد
یا مات شوـے یا بری یابرند

Dar kooy-e kharaabaat, takabbor nakharand
Mardi, besar-e-kooy-e kharaabaat, barand
Aanjaa cho resee, moghaameree baayad kard
Yaa maat shavee, yaa bebaree, yaa bebarand

in the | alley of | ruins/selflessness | arrogance | they
    won't buy
manliness/lack of pretention/self-respect | in the alley of |
    ruins | they take (they honor these qualities)
there | when | you reach | gambling | [one] has to | do
either | checkmate | you become | or | you win |
    or | they win

*I*n the alley of selflessness, arrogance has no value.
What sells the best is self-respect and honesty.
When you get there be prepared to gamble
For either you are checkmated and they win, or you win.

678 AK

*I*n the tavern of love such drunkards—who has seen?
Barrels all broken and scattered about—who has seen?
The ground and the ceiling of heaven are full of wine,
But a cup in anyone's hand—who has seen?

684 AK

*W*hen a darvish spills the secrets of the world
With his every word, he bestows great lands and palaces.
The darvish is not the person who begs his way through
The darvish is the one who surrenders his life in
    one asking.

686 AK

Samaa has made our hearts addicted to turning.
Like the spring clouds, it has filled us with lightning.
O Venus, the source of pleasures, open up your generous
   palm
For the musicians and the clapping hands have no breath
   left to move.

700 AK

In the end, the mountains of imagination were nothing
   but a house.
And this grand life of mine was nothing but an excuse.
You've been hearing my story so patiently for a lifetime
Now hear this: it was nothing but a fairy tale.

704 AK

I went to the house of the master of union
He came out toward me, laughing.
Pulled me in His arms sweet as sugar cubes,
Saying, "Salaam, O lover, O Sufi, O man of science."

711 AK

*T*he day that I am crazy for your love,
I'll be such a madman that even demons can not compare.
What a blink of your eyelashes does to my heart,
Even the stroke of the pen of the master of Divan can
    not compare.

720 AK

Your prison is more pleasing than freedom.
Your curse is more pleasing than sugar candy.
The strike of your sword is more pleasing than life.
To receive your fatal wound is more pleasing than
     eternal health.

728 AK

The lovers crawl in and out of your alley,
They bathe in drips of blood; and not finding you,
     they give up and leave.
I am forever stationed at your door like the earth,
While others come and go like the wind.

731 UT

There is a king who is aware of every mask you put on.
Whether you keep silent or wail, he is aware.
Everyone desires to stand up and lecture,
I am the servant of the one who honors silence.

742 AK

Alas, don't say those treading the path are not the
    chosen ones,
That the followers of Christ, or the faithless are not
    the chosen ones —
Because you are not chosen to be the keeper of secrets,
You think that others are not the chosen ones.

745 UT

*A*ny lifetime that is spent without seeing the master
Is either death in disguise or deep sleep.
The water that pollutes you is poison;
The poison that purifies you is water.

750 UT

*W*hen his lips are full of anger
Sweetness rains down in the two worlds.
If you see a moon in the cave of your heart
Hear it from me, it is Shams-e Tabriz.

759 UT

Love is from the infinite, and will remain until eternity.
The seeker of love escapes the chains of birth and death.
Tomorrow, when resurrection comes,
The heart that is not in love will fail the test.

764 AK

You called Him a moon—you are mistaken. How can
    the moon compare?
You called Him a king—you are wrong. How can
    a king compare?
How often do you say, "You get up late."
When the Sun is with me, does time have any meaning?

776 UT

I am in love with you, what good is advice?
I have tasted poison, what good is sugar?
They say, "Fasten a rope around his feet."
It's the heart that is crazy, what good is in tying
    up my feet?

788 UT

*A*ny person passing by my grave will become drunk.
    If he stops there, for eternity he will become drunk.
    If he goes into the ocean, the ocean and the shore
        will become drunk.
    If he goes into the grave, the tomb will become drunk.

791 UT

*U*ntil a disciple annihilates himself completely,
Union will not be revealed to him.
Union can not be penetrated. It is your own destruction.
Otherwise, every worthless person would become
    the truth.

800 UT

*W*ithout love, there will be no joy and no festivity in
    the world.
Without love, there will be no true living and no harmony.
If a hundred raindrops pour down from the clouds
    to the sea
Without love's doing, a pearl will not form in the
    deepest waters.

805 UT

Who says that the immortal one has died? *
Who says that the Sun of hope has died?
Look, it is the enemy of the Sun who has come to the
    roof top!
Closing both eyes shut, crying, "O, the Sun has died!"
    *(Referring to the disappearance of Shams)

806 AK

I was all tied up yet another rope was added.
I had lost my heart to grief, yet another sorrow was added.
I was caught in the curl of His hair
Around my neck yet another noose was added.

809 AK

Today the Beloved is asking for madness.
I am already mad, yet He wants even more lunacy.
If this is not so, then why is He rending the veils?
I am disgraced already yet He wants it all revealed.

813 UT

The men of the path who know the secrets of the unknown,
Are hidden from the sight of the narrow-minded ones.
Have you seen anything more strange? The ones who
    reach the truth
Become believers, but the people call them infidels.

814 AK

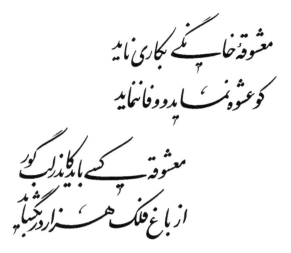

Ma'shoogheye khaanegi, bekaari naayad
Koo eshveh namaayad-o, vafaa nanmaayad
Ma'shogh-e kasee baayad, kaandar lab-e goor
Az baagh-e falak, hezaar dar bogshaayad

the mistress/lover of | the house | for any job | she is not
   good
for she | coquetry/tease | she does | faithful/devoted |
   she is not
the lover | a person | it should be | who | at the | tip of |
   the grave
from | the garden of | the sky | a thousand | door[s] |
   she will open

The mistress of the house is good for nothing,
All she does is play foolish games.
The true mistress is the one who, when you are at the tip
   of the grave,
From the garden of the sky she will open a thousand
   doors of the horizon.

824 AK

Behold O tired heart, the relief has come.
Sweetly take a breath, for the great one has come.
The Lover, who takes care of the lover's needs,
In the form of a human being, to this world He has come.

840 AK

The more my heart seeks His approval,
The more He speaks with the sharp edge of a sword.
Look! There is blood dripping from His finger tips.
Why is He washing His hands in my blood?

842 AK

O heart, the morning glory in a dark night who has seen?
A true lover with a good reputation who has seen?
You cry out that I have burned
Cry not, a burned, still unbaked, who has seen?

844 UT

*T*he dust of your door from the water of Kosar is
　　more pleasant.
On your path, my feet from my head, are more pleasant.
When the sound of the drum of your love was heard
　　by the moon
The moon became two and said, "This way orbiting
　　is more pleasant."

876 AK

O man of Samaa, keep your stomach empty.
The ney cries so bitterly because it is empty inside.
When you fill your belly with too much pastry
Then you will be deprived of the Lover, His kisses,
    and all.

882 AK

When my poetic nature found life through the repetition
    of God's name,
The goddess of poetry entered the house of the mind.
It created a thousand maidens in every verse
Every one, pure like Mary, pregnant yet still a virgin.

906 AK

God revealed to the Prophet a divine inspiration.
He said, "Don't settle, don't tread except in the alley
    of the lovers."
It may be that the universe is warmed by your flame
But listen, while speaking of the ash the fire dies away.

907 AK

Without you, I plant roses, yet only thorns grow.
A snake comes out of the peacock's egg.
I hold a rubaab, it sounds like a tar.
And if I play it, even the eight heavens will burn
    in flames.

910 AK

I said, "My eyes." He said, "Focus them on his path
   of arrival."
I said, "My guts." He said, "Tear them open."
I said, "My heart." He said, "What do you have
   in your heart."
I said, "Your sorrow." He said, "Keep it."

912 AK

I said, "Tell me what to do?" He said, "Die."
I said, "I am becoming lighter, impurities are vanishing."
   He said, "Die."
I said, "I'll become a candle, a butterfly,
O Your face, is my bright candle." He said, "Die."

930 UT

O heart, let go of all your clothes and throw them
    on the path.
Think of it as the shirt of Joseph, let it cover your face.
You are a small fish, you have no life without water.
Don't think, just throw yourself into this stream.

936 AK

O tulip, come and learn from my face the vibrancy of color.
And O Venus, come and learn from my heart the sound
    of the harp.
When the inner sound of union plays its song,
O eternal fate, come and learn its sweet melody.

942 AK

*I*t's turned night and I have no news of night and day.
Seeing His sun-like face, my nights have become
   bright like days.
O night, you are dark because you are ignorant
   of His glory
O daylight, go and learn from Him what it means
   to shine.

956 UT

I have come again to set a blazing fire
To repentance, sin, crime, and discrimination.
I have brought a flame which is proclaiming
"Anything that is not of god, depart from the path."

968 UT

Of the games of this evolving world, don't be afraid.
Of what is coming to you, whatever your fortune, don't
    be afraid.
Make the most of this single breath called life.
Don't think of what is gone, and of the future don't
    be afraid.

977 AK

Since you are not a lover, go and spin wool instead.
Go and do a hundred works of a hundred types
    in a hundred professions.
If there is no wine of love in your skull
Then go and lick the bowls in the kitchen of lovers.

988 AK

That hidden mendicant has been revealed.
Seek traces of his feet in the light of my eyes.
He is God or he has been sent by God.
O the musician of the soul, stay with me for one breath.

996 AK

O love, transform the character of these sour people.
O backbone of the world, show kindness to the seekers
    of beauty.
Will it become less the garden of your face,
If from the apple of your chin, you offer two or three
    peaches?

1004 UT

Last night I saw Him seated in a gathering.
I could not hold Him in my arms,
So I placed my face near His, as an excuse,
As if I were whispering some holy words in His ear.

1012 UT

O heart, do worry about your destiny.
In this world of alienation, come and join our gathering.
If you desire to mount the breeze-of-dawn and ride
    into eternity
Then become the dust of the feet of the horse of a darvish.

1012 AK

$\mathcal{A}$t times I called Him wine, at times a cup.
　At times a polished gold, at times a rough silver.
　At times a bait, at times a prey, and sometimes a trap.
　All this a mystery until I reveal His name.

1019 UT

$\mathcal{Y}$ou said, "How are you?" Come, for I am as happy
　　as daylight.
Like day, I bring an end to myself, and in joy I start all
　　over again.
When I saw your fiery face I became like wild rue
Burning in your flames, burning, I am burning so joyfully.

1026 UT

Constantly serve the truth and you will become eternal.
Lose yourself in excitement and the frenzy of true love.
Boil like the wine in the barrel of your body
Then see yourself becoming the divine companion and
    the Saaqi.

1028 AK

Last night in retreat I was talking to the master
    of knowledge.
I said, "Please don't keep the secrets of the world
    from me."
Ever so gracefully he whispered in my ear,
"This is something to be seen, not to be talked about.
    Be silent."

1035 UT

امروز سماعت و سماعت و سماع

نورست و شعاعت و شعاعت و شعاع

این عشق مشاعت و مشاعت و مشاع

از عقل وداعت و وداعت و وداع

Emrooz samaa'ast-o, samaa'ast-o, samaa
Noorast-o shoaa'ast-o, shoaa'ast-o, shoaa
Een eshgh, moshaa'ast-o, moshaa'ast-o, moshaa
Az agh'l vedaa'ast-o, vedaa'ast-o vedaa

today | it is samaa and | it is samaa and | samaa
it is light and | it is illumination and | it is illumination
    and | illumination
this | love | it is unifying | it is unifying | unifying
of | intellect | it is bidding farewell and | it is bidding
    farewell and | farewell

Today it's time for samaa, for samaa, for samaa.
Today is bright and illuminating, illuminating,
    illuminating.
This love is unifying, unifying, unifying.
And it's bidding the intellect farewell, farewell, farewell.

1046 UT

The nightingale came to the garden, so we can escape
   the raven.
It is you who brings us to the garden. O light of our eyes.
Like a lily, we open up and unravel from ourselves.
Like a flowing stream, we go from one garden to the next.

1055 AK

In the waters of purity, I melted like salt
Neither blasphemy, nor faith, nor conviction, nor
   doubt remained.
In the center of my heart a star has appeared
And all the seven heavens have become lost in it.

1070 UT

$\mathcal{F}$or a while I lived amongst the people,
Never truly sensing the smell of graciousness, the color
   of kindness.
It is better that I hide myself again,
Like water in iron, like fire in stone.

1082 AK

$\mathcal{T}$his love is perfection, perfection, perfection.
The passions are imaginary, imaginary, imaginary.
This light is full of glory, glory, glory.
This is the day of unity, unity, unity.

1083 UT

$\mathcal{Q}$uestioning will not reveal the mysteries of the truth,
Nor giving away one's goods and properties.
Unless the vision and the heart have suffered five years
    of bloody torment
From mere chatter, no one will walk on the path
    of selflessness.

1088 AK

$\mathcal{Y}$ou have asked of me gold and heart, O heart-breaker.
Truly, I have neither this, nor is the other possible.
What gold? When gold? From where gold? A poor man
    and gold?
What heart? When heart? From where heart? A lover
    and heart?

1091 UT

This world is teeming with the presence of Christ
Where then can the garb of an Anti-Christ fit?
Where can fit the bitter juice of a dark heart
When the sack of the world is bursting with
    crystalline water?

1091 AK

A perfect love and a heart-stealer of such beauty.
A heart full of words and the tongue a wordless mute.
Have you heard a legend as rare as this?
Dying of thirst and next to me flows crystalline water.

1099 AK

Like a snake, spellbound, I am twisting and winding.
Like a strand of the Beloved's hair, I am twisting
and winding.
I swear, I have no idea what kind of twisting and winding
this is,
I know this, if I don't twist and wind, I do not exist.

1135 UT

I will come out of this creation as the Creator
And I won't hold my tongue any longer.
Since the cremating kitchen of the truth is bursting with
naked bodies
How much longer should I be satisfied with just plain
warm water?

1135 AK

O life and the world, I have lost both life and the world.
O bright Moon, I have lost the earth and the sky.
Don't place more wine in my hand, pour it in my mouth.
I am so drunk on you that I have lost the way to my
   mouth.

1159 AK

Do you think I am in command here?
Do you think that even a single breath belongs to me?
I am like a pen in the hand of a writer, who is indeed
   myself
Like a polo stick, surrendered to the polo master,
   who is me.

1167 UT

I smell the fragrance of your mouth in the grass.
I see the color of your face in the lily and jasmine.
Even without these, I just open my lips
And hear your name being repeated over and over again.

1182 AK

I am out of work but your love's sorrow is my new duty.
In these jobless days I am planting the seeds of devotion.
Night and day I carve the immaculate face of union
With my imagination, like a chip axe, as if I were a
    carpenter.

1186 AK

*U*ntil you abandon your own desires, I won't give in.
Until you accept my commands, I won't give in.
Stop your cheap tricks, stop playing dead all the time.
I swear on your life until you are dead, I won't give in.

1190 AK

*Y*our love lifts my soul from the body to the sky
And you lift me up out of the two worlds.
I want your sun to reach my raindrops,
So your heat can raise my soul upward like a cloud.

1028 UT

$\mathcal{A}$ll the time before, my talk was only madness.
And I complained about this and that.
For a lifetime I pounded this door, and when they
    opened it
I saw I had been pounding from the inside.

1249 AK

$\mathcal{T}$oday I'll do an intoxicating samaa
And out of my skull I will form a cup.
Today I am walking about drunk in this town
Seeking an intellectual, so I can turn him mad.

1254 UT

A poet I am not, and poetry doesn't provide my livelihood.
I don't boast about excellence for it doesn't concern me.
My art and excellence are but a single cup
And unless it's from the Beloved's hand I won't even
    touch it.

1256 AK

I see so deeply within myself.
Not needing my eyes, I can see everything clearly.
Why would I want to bother my eyes again
Now that I see the world through His eyes?

1261 UT

The sweetheart came in and found me tired and sad.
He smiled, walked toward me and sat by my side.
Scratching my head, he said, "O my poor...,
It's not so good, seeing you like this."

1265 UT

My kerchief, my cape and my turban—all three
Were appraised at a very small amount.
Haven't you heard my name throughout the world?
I am a nobody, a nobody, a nobody.

1284 UT

If you show patience, I'll rid you of this virtue.
If you fall asleep, I'll rub the sleep from your eyes.
If you become a mountain, I'll melt you in fire
And if you become an ocean, I'll drink all your water.

1287 AK

I touch the soil of your threshold with my head.
My heart is tangled by the lockets of your dark hair.
Life has reached up to my lips—bring your lips next
    to mine
So at last I could place my life into your sweet mouth.

1289 UT

ما کار و دکان و پیشه را سوخته‌ایم
شعر و غزل و دو بیتی آموخته‌ایم

در عشق، که او جان و دل و دیده ماست
جان و دل و دیده، هر سه را سوخته‌ایم

Maa kaar-o dokaan-o peesheraa, sookhte-eem
She'er-o ghazal-o dobeitee, aamookhte-eem
Dar eshgh, keh oo jaan-o del-o deedeye maast
Jaan-o del-o deedeh, har seraa sookhte-eem

We | work and | store and | craft | have burned
poetry and | love songs and | couplets | have learned
in | love | which | he [is] | soul and | heart and |
    vision of | ours
soul and | heart and | vision | all | the three | have burned

*W*e have set blaze to our work, store, and profession.
We have learned instead poetry, love songs, and couplets.
In love, He is our heart, soul, and vision;
Heart, soul and vision, we have set blaze to all three.

1293 UT

$\mathcal{A}$t times we seem disturbed on the path of union.
At times we scorch in the fire of the pain of separation.
When this illusion of you-and-I disappears from me-
   and-you
Then me-and-you, without the veil of you-and-I, will
   live in bliss together.

1301 AK

$\mathcal{F}$or a while, at a young age, I became a master.
For a while, I was happy at the sight of friends.
Now, listen to the end of my legend, see what happened –
I came in like a cloud, and I left like a wind.

1303 UT

We are celebrating, don't come to us without a daf.
Get up and play the drum, for we are victorious.
We are drunk, but not drunk on grape's wine;
Anything you can think of, we are far, far from that.

1322 UT

This is me: Sometimes hidden and sometimes revealed,
Sometimes a devoted Muslim, sometimes a Hebrew
and a Christian.
For me to fit inside everyone's heart,
I put on a new face everyday.

1325 AK

O Beloved, accept me and liberate my soul.
Intoxicate me and liberate me from the two worlds.
If I set my heart on anything but you,
Let fire burn my inside and liberate me on that too.

1372 UT

*A*t the moment of death when the soul has used up
   the body,
It drops the limp corpse like a worn out rag.
This body of dust is returned back to dust
And the soul, through its pure ageless light, creates
   another body.

1431 UT

O pure soul, it is sorrow that refines you.
O holy body, it is sorrow that obliterates you.
This fire of love that you are burning in
Will be your garden of paradise.

1449 UT

Hold on to yourself, lose my intimacy, even if you
     are with me.
You are a great distance away from me.
You won't reach me until you merge with me
In the path of love, either "you" remain or "I."

1475 UT

He stole my heart last night with a hundred love spells
He opened my chest and found it was full of blood.
He said, "Place him in the fire for a while."
Which means, he is still unbaked, that is why he is so
    full of blood.

1506 UT

Go and choose pain, choose pain, choose pain.
I have no answer to the problem, except pain.
Don't feel lonely, don't say you have no companions.
It is the lack of pain that calls for real concern.

1515 UT

The books of Egypt and Bagdad, O soul,
I have filled with my cries and screams, O soul.
An hour of love is worth more than a hundred worlds—
Let a hundred lives be offered to love, O soul.

1515 AK

One day I said our souls are one—
I will never be without you again.
I know you win everything I lose—
I lose, so that I can stay with you.

1526 UT

When your chest is free of your limiting ego,
Then you will see the ageless Beloved.
You can not see yourself without a mirror;
Look at the Beloved, He is the brightest mirror.

1552 UT

In the alley of your imagination, what are you searching for?
Why are you washing your face with blood-stained tears?
From the crown of your head to your toes, all is possessed
    by the truth;
O you, ignorant of your true self, what are you looking for?

1557 UT

O you who have died, taking to the grave the desire
    to undo your knot.
You were born in union yet died in separation.
You have fallen asleep, thirsty at the edge of a
    mountain spring,
You have died of poverty, on top of a treasure.

1601 UT

O Lord, don't tempt me with the senses.
Don't play me with anything that is not you.
I go toward you, escaping from the seduction of myself,
I am all yours—don't give me back to myself again.

1606 UT

Do you know what night is? Listen, O wise one:
First, keep the lovers away from outsiders.
Tonight is very special, for the moon is our housemate!
I am drunk, the moon is in love, and the night is
    totally mad.

1634 UT

I said, "You are the wine, and I am the cup,
I am dead and you are the source of life
Now open the door of devotion." He said, "Quiet
Would anyone let a madman loose in the house?"

1636 UT

I am the mirror and I am the face
I am drunk by the saucer of infinity
I am the repeller of torture and I am the healing
I am the water of life and its carrying vessel.

1652 AK

*J*oyfully, joyfully, O my idol, you have come with yet
    a new face!
Laughingly, you have come with lips of rarest rubies!
That day when you took my heart from my chest,
    it wasn't enough—
For today you have come again, asking for my life.

1662 UT

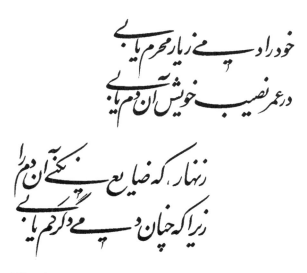

Khod-raa cho damee zeyaar, mahram yaabee
Dar omr-e naseeb-e kheesh, aan dam yaabee
Zanhaar, keh zaaye' nakonee aan dam-raa
Zeeraa keh cheneen damee, degar kam yaabee

yourself | when | a breath/moment | with the lover |
    in close relation | you find
in the | life of | portion of | yourself | that |
    breath/moment | you find
alas | that | damage/spoiled | you don't do | that breath/
    moment
because | that | of this nature | breath/moment | again |
    a few | you find

*W*hen you find yourself with the Beloved, embracing for
    one breath,
In that moment you will find your true destiny.
Alas, don't spoil this precious moment
Moments like this are very, very rare.

1667 UT

O moon, you have risen and become bright.
You have danced, twirling around the heavens.
When you learn that you are one with the Truth
Like Truth itself, you too will vanish from peoples' sight.

1680 UT

Last night you slept and left me alone.
And tonight, pretending to be asleep, you toss in
    all directions.
I thought you and I are one until the day of resurrection—
What happened to your drunken promises?

1683 UT

I asked you for one kiss, you gave me six.
You are such a master! Whose student have you been?
How great is the goodness and generosity you have
　　created!
Now, because of you, a thousand souls in this world
　　are free.

1692 UT

I was a particle, you made me greater than a mountain
I was always behind, you made me the leader of all.
You made me the cure for wounded hearts, lost in rapture
You made me dance to my own clapping, in ecstasy.

1709 UT

You made me the goal of travelers on the path of religion
And the trusted beholder of faith.
I said, "I am weak, and this load is too heavy."
You gave me strength and made me like a mountain
    of iron.

1715 UT

Even if your days of union with the Beloved are in
    the hundreds,
The soul will not become content with the wailing
    of the heart.
O you who are laughing at this discourse,
Haven't you reached madness yet? Are you still holding
    on to your intellect?

1729 UT

This is you, making me drunk in a monastery,
Turning me into an idol-worshipper while I am seated
    in Ka'be.
I have no control in this game of good and bad
I am in your hands, awaiting your gentle control.

1745 UT

This is you: A hundred intercessions and a hundred
    lamentations.
I want to kiss your feet, but you will not let me.
Give me water, give me fire—regardless of what you
    give me,
You are the Sultan and the ruler of all lands.

1758 UT

O you who desire the world, you are just a hired slave.
And you in love with paradise, you are far from the Truth.
You who are happy with the two worlds out of ignorance,
You have not experienced the happiness of His sorrow,
     you are excused.

1788 UT

F or your love, there is someone in every corner staying
     up till dawn
Night is sifting amber from your locks of hair.
The painter of eternity is painting images in every
     direction.
He is painting Tabriz, for the sake of my heart's comfort.

1804 UT

$\mathcal{A}$ll I do is wrong, but you are my good action
    and that's enough.
The desire of this lifetime of love's intoxication is you,
    and that's enough.
I know when I decide to leave this body
People will ask, "What has he done?" The answer is you
    and that's enough.

                          1812 UT

$\mathcal{U}$ntil you've found pain, you won't reach the cure
Until you've given up life, you won't unite with
    the supreme soul
Until you've found fire inside yourself, like the Friend,
You won't reach the spring of life, like Khezr.

                          1815 UT

How long will you think about this painful life?
How long will you think about this harmful world?
The only thing it can take from you is your body.
Don't say all this rubbish and stop thinking.

1828 UT

You will lose your life on our path if you are a man
    of the heart
If not, hold your head in grief, you are pardoned by us.
That land cannot be found through doubt—
It is like seeking the truth while being stuck in mud!

1842 UT

I travelled in the desert of your love
Hoping to find a word about uniting with you.
In every house I entered,
I saw bodies scattered about and heads fallen to the floor.

1854 AK

*I*f you are in search of the place of the soul, you are the soul.
If you are in search of a morsel of bread, you are the bread.
If you know this secret, then you know
That whatever you seek, you are that.

1864 UT

There is a candle in the heart of man, waiting to be kindled.
In separation from the Friend, there is a cut waiting
    to be stitched.
O, you who are ignorant of endurance and the burning
    fire of love—
Love comes of its own free will, it can't be learned
    in any school.

1881 UT

You can bring tears to these eyes by striking them
    with thorns,
You can make this heart, weak as a string of hair,
    the target of your arrows of unkindness
I will not let loose of your garb
Even if you hit my face, like a daf, a thousand times.

1888 UT

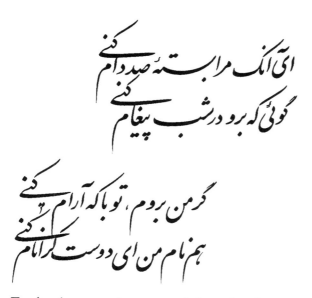

Ey Aank maraa, basteye sad daam koni
Gooyee ke, "Boro" Dar shab, peighaam koni
Gar man beravam, to baa ke aaraam koni?
Ham naam-e man ey doost, keraa naam koni?

O | you that | to me | bonded/tied up of | a hundred |
    trap you do
you say | that | go | in the night | message/page |
    you do/send
if | I | go | you | with | whom | calm/relax/rest | you do
same | name of | me | O | friend/Beloved | which person
    | name | you do/call

You tie me up to a hundred traps.
You send me messages in the night to leave you alone.
If I go, who will make you feel safe and warm?
O Beloved, who has the same name as me? Who will
    come when you call?

1895 UT

I am the wind and you are a leaf. If you don't shake,
    what will you do?
I grant a task. If you don't perform, what will you do?
When I break your pitcher with a thrown stone,
If a hundred seas and a hundred treasures don't pour out,
    what will you do?

1900 UT

*N*either I am me nor you are you nor you are me.
Also, I am me you are you and you are me.
I am so close to you, O, my Mongolian mistress
That I am confused whether I am you or you are me.

905 UT

I said, "How are you, my moon, are you happy?
    Are you sad?"
Moon said, "Should anyone ask of my condition?
This is the countenance of the moon,
Radiating a soft, harmonious and healing glow."

1908 UT

O my soul, would I ever become fed up with you?
    No, no, no.
Would I ever take another lover but you? No, no, no.
In your garden of union, when all I see are roses,
Would I ever rush toward the thorns? No, no, no.

1915 UT

You personify God's message.
You reflect the King's face.
There is nothing in the universe that you are not
Everything you want, look for it within yourself—
    you are that.

1921 UT

O wise one, you inflate with every little fantasy
For no good reason, you turn sour or become happy
I see you amidst the flames yet I let you stay
Until you become baked, shrewd, and a master yourself.

1923 UT

The soul is like a snake during the day and like a
    fish at night
Open your eyes and realize which is your travelling
    companion.
At times you are with Haroot the Sorcerer, deep in a well
At times you reside in the heart of Venus, watching over
    the Moon.

1937 UT

You are wearing a turban and you won't give it
    to the musicians
Give away that turban and let your pride go with it!
Rescue yourself from what you have no control over!
Give that turban and in return receive the crown of a king.

1938 UT

*O*h, sound of rubaab, where are you coming from?
You are so fiery, tempting, and full of turmoil,
You are the spy of the heart and the messenger
    of heavenly lands
Whatever sound you make is the secret of the heart.

1945 UT

*L*ast night the Beloved came to my door frenzied with love
I said, "Go away. Tonight you are not coming in." ,
On His way out He said: "So this is your devotion,
The world has come to your door, and you don't open it."

1950 UT

γou said, "You are mad and have the disposition
    of a lunatic."
You are mad yourself, for you are asking wisdom from me.
You said, "How shameless! You show no trace of
    emotions."
A mirror always shows the absolute truth.

1977 UT

GLOSSARY OF TERMS

Daf: A kind of frame drum.

Darvish: (Dervish) A Persian word for one who has renounced the world. Certain darvish orders of Iran trace their heritage back to the pre-Zoroastrian order of the *Mirtha*. Their system of belief is based upon rigorous exercises, devotional movements, chants, proper diet, meditation, whirling and non-attachment to the material properties of the world. They also see a distinct difference between a darvish and a Sufi, although in many mystical orders of Islam the words *darvish* and *Sufi* are used interchangeably.

Divan: A master poet's collection of poems.

Ka'ba: The Muslim place of pilgrimage. A cubed-shape shrine in the city of Mecca, Saudi Arabia.

Khaneghah: A Sufi monastery.

Khezr: The immortal Green-Being, mentioned in the Koran. Some believe the vision of Khezr alone grants the seeker immortality.

Mansoor: Mansoor Hallaj also known as Mansoor Mastaane. A tenth-century Sufi martyr. He was crucified for proclaiming these words: *"Anal Hagh"* (I am the truth).

Moulana: Our master. Rumi's title.

Ney: An end-blown bamboo flute. One of Rumi's favorite instruments.

The Prophet: Muhammad, founder of Islam.

Rubaab: A kind of lute played in Afghanistan.

Rumi: His full name is Moulana Jalaluddin Mohammad Ebne Sheikh Bahauddin Mohammad Ebne Housseine Balkhi. The family name of Khatibi was also used by his father and grandfather. Born in Persia, in the city of Balkh (in modern day Afghanistan) on September 30, 1207, and passed away in Konya (in today's Turkey) on December 17, 1273. The Persians named him Rumi (the Roman) mainly because of the close proximity of Konya to the Byzantine Empire. Rumi was one of the most important figures of the thirteenth century, and has been called the greatest mystical poet of any age. Others have said that he can be compared in stature only to such Westerners as Dante and Shakespeare. He completed two epic collections of poems, each consisting of about 35,000 verses. The first is *Divan-e Shams-e Tabriz* (the collective poems of Shams of Tabriz) which is a collection of passionate poems mainly addressed to God and to Shams as a vehicle for God's energy. The second is *Massnavi* (also spelled Mathnawi, his most famous work) which is a collection of guiding words for the students of mysticism. He is the national poet of these three countries, Iran, Afghanistan and Turkey.

Saaghi: Cupbearer. In the poetry of Rumi, Saaghi is the metaphor for the moment one is enraptured by a divinely induced state of ecstasy. When one is experiencing this state, one says that the Saaghi has brought the wine of love.

Samaa: In the poetry of Rumi, *samaa* refers to the whirling dance of the darvishes. This sacred movement is offered to and symbolizes the constant movement of the universe. The smallest atoms to the galaxies all are subject to rotation. Darvishes believe that the human body is no exception, and through whirling one harmonizes with the energy of the creation.

Shams of Tabriz: His full name is Shamsuddin Mohammad Ebne Ali Ebne Molkdaad. Rumi's spiritual friend who became the conduit for transformation for Rumi, and because of this Rumi revered him. Shams also means the sun.

Sufi: The mystical branch of Islam. Sufism traces its origins to Prophet Mohammad and his son-in-law Imam Ali. Some Sufi orders consider Ali to be the first Sufi. In many spiritual orders of Islam the words Sufi and darvish are used interchangeably.

Tar: A Persian lute.

Two worlds: Here and hereafter. This world and the next.

Water of life: The inner nectar of immortality. The nectar that holds the essence of the creation. Described as a spring that one encounters in meditation.

PERSIAN MYSTICAL TERMS

Beloved: God, perceived as one's closest friend, companion, and a lover. A universal mystical concept.

Breeze: The life-giving breath of the Beloved.

Burning: The pain that follows the process of spiritual growth and purification.

Desert: The universe, the plain of consciousness that needs to be crossed so one can attain self-realization.

Drunkenness: Being enraptured by the love of God. A divinely induced feeling of ecstasy.

Garden: A metaphor for a beautiful and a harmonious state of being. Also used literally as a flower field.

Hair: The state of being in the Beloved's presence has been described as being caught in the Beloved's beautiful net-like hair. It can also mean illusion.

Killing: The destruction of one's ego, and its limited sense of identity. It especially refers to the breaking of one's attachment to the physical body.

King: God, the Beloved.

Nightingale: The soul singing to the Beloved.

Ocean: The universe, the plain of consciousness that needs to be crossed so one can attain self-realization.

Pearl: Represents maturation and compilation of one's character.

Rose: The eternal and perfect beauty of the Beloved. In Rumi's poetry the word thorn is used as the opposite of rose.

Sea: The universe, the plain of consciousness that needs to be crossed for one to attain self-realization.

Sorrow: The pain of being away from one's loved one. In the poetry of Rumi, the pain of separation from God.

Wedding Night: The night the soul (lover) joins in union with God (the Beloved). It also refers to the day a great saint leaves his body.

Wine: Nectar of love, divinely intoxicating presence of the Beloved.

BIBLIOGRAPHY

Furuzanfar, Badiuzzaman, *Kulliyat-e Shams-e Tabrizi*. Tehran: Amir Kabir Press, 12th edition, 1988.

Furuzanfar, Badiuzzaman, *Kulliyat-e Shams*. Tehran: University of Tehran, First Edition, 1963, Vol. 8.

ADDITIONAL TITLES FROM HOHM PRESS

FOR LOVE OF THE DARK ONE: SONGS OF MIRABAI
Revised edition
Translations and Introduction by Andrew Schelling

Mirabai is probably the best known poet in India today, even though she lived 400 years ago (1498-1593). Her poems are ecstatic declarations of surrender to and praise of Krishna, whom she lovingly calls "The Dark One." Mira's poetry is as alive today as it was in the sixteenth century—poetry of freedom, of breaking with traditional stereotypes, of trusting completely in the benediction of God. It is also some of the most exalted mystical poetry in all of world literature, expressing her complete surrender to the Divine, her longing, and her madness in love. This revised edition contains the original 80 poems, a completely revised Introduction, updated glossary, bibliography and discography, and additional Sanskrit notations

Paper, 128 pages, $12.00   ISBN: 0-934252-84-X

• • •

THE WAY OF POWER
by Red Hawk

Red Hawk's poetry cuts close to the bone whether he is telling humorous tales or indicting the status-quo throughout the culture. Touching upon themes of life and death, power, devotion and adoration, these eighty new poems reveal the poet's deep concern for all of life, and particularly for the needs of women, children and the earth

"This is such a strong book. Red Hawk is like Whitman: he says what he sees…" William Packard, editor, *New York Quarterly*.

Paper, 96 pages, $10.00   ISBN: 0-934252-64-X

**TO ORDER PLEASE SEE ACCOMPANYING ORDER FORM
OR CALL 1-800-381-2700 TO PLACE YOUR ORDER NOW.**

ADDITIONAL TITLES FROM HOHM PRESS

THE ONLY GRACE IS LOVING GOD
by Lee Lozowick

Love, God, Loving God, Grace, Divine Will—these subjects have engaged the minds and hearts of theologians throughout the ages, and even caused radical schisms within organized religions. Lee Lozowick dares to address them again, and in a way entirely original. He challenges all conventional definitions of love, and all superficial assumptions about the nature of loving God, and introduces a radical distinction, which he calls the "whim of God," to explain why the random and beneficent Grace of loving God is humanity's ultimate possibility. More than just esoteric musings, *The Only Grace is Loving God* is an urgent and practical appeal to every hungry heart.

Paper, 108 pages, $5.95   ISBN: 0-934252-07-6

• • •

MARROW OF FLAME: Poems of the Spiritual Journey
by Dorothy Walters
Foreword by Andrew Harvey

This compilation of 105 new poems documents and celebrates the author's interior journey of kundalini awakening. Her poems cut through the boundaries of religious provincialism to the essence of longing, love and union that supports every authentic spiritual tradition, as she writes of the Mother Goddess, as well as of Krishna, Rumi, Bodhidharma, Hildegard of Bingen, and many others.Best-selling spiritual author and poet Andrew Harvey has written the book's Introduction. His commentary illuminates aspects of Dorothy's spiritual life and highlights the "unfailing craft" of her poems.

"Dorothy Walters writes poetry that speaks to us from the heart to the heart, gently touching our deepest spiritual stirrings."—Riane Eisler, author, *The Chalice and the Blade.*

Paper, 144 pages, $12.00   ISBN: 0-934252-96-3

TO ORDER PLEASE SEE ACCOMPANYING ORDER FORM OR CALL 1-800-381-2700 TO PLACE YOUR ORDER NOW.

ADDITIONAL TITLES FROM HOHM PRESS

GRACE AND MERCY IN HER WILD HAIR
Selected Poems to the Mother Goddess
by Ramprasad Sen; Translated by Leonard Nathan and Clinton Seely

Ramprasad Sen, a great devotee of the Mother Goddess, composed these passionate poems in 18th-century Bengal, India. His lyrics are songs of praise or sorrowful laments addressed to the great goddesses Kali and Tara, guardians of the cycles of birth and death.

Paper, 120 pages, $12.00   ISBN 0-934252-94-7

• • •

THE ALCHEMY OF TRANSFORMATION
by Lee Lozowick
Foreword by Claudio Naranjo, M.D.

"I really appreciate Lee's message. The world needs to hear his God-talk. It's insightful and healing."—John White, author, and editor, *What is Enlightenment?: Exploring the Goal of the Spiritual Path.*

A concise and straightforward overview of the principles of spiritual life as developed and taught by Lee Lozowick for the past twenty years in the West. Subjects of use to seekers and serious students of any spiritual tradition include: • From self-centeredness to God-centeredness • The role of a Teacher and a practice in spiritual life • The job of the community in "self"-liberation • Longing and devotion. Lee Lozowick's spiritual tradition is that of the western Baul, related in teaching and spirit to the Bauls of Bengal, India. *The Alchemy of Transformation* presents his radical, elegant and irreverent approach to human alchemical transformation.

Paper, 192 pages, $14.95   ISBN: 0-934252-62-9

**TO ORDER PLEASE SEE ACCOMPANYING ORDER FORM
OR CALL 1-800-381-2700 TO PLACE YOUR ORDER NOW.**

ADDITIONAL TITLES FROM HOHM PRESS

THE MIRROR OF THE SKY
Songs of the Bauls of Bengal
Translated by Deben Bhattacharya

Baul music today is prized by world musicologists, and Baul lyrics are treasured by readers of ecstatic and mystical poetry. Baul music, lyrics, and accompanying dance reflect the passion, the devotion and the iconoclastic freedom of this remarkable sect of musicians and lovers of the Divine, affectionately known as "God's troubadours."

The Mirror of the Sky is a translation of 204 songs, including an extensive introduction to the history and faith of the Bauls, and the composition of their music. It includes a CD of authentic Baul artists, recorded as much as forty years ago by Bhattacharya, a specialist in world music. The current CD is a rare presentation of this infrequently documented genre.

Paper, 288 pages, $24.95 (includes CD)   ISBN: 0-934252-89-0
CD sold separately, $16.95

• • •

THE WOMAN AWAKE: Feminine Wisdom for Spiritual Life
by Regina Sara Ryan

Through the stories and insights of great women of spirit whom the author has met or been guided by in her own journey, this book highlights many faces of the Divine Feminine: the silence, the solitude, the service, the power, the compassion, the art, the darkness, the sexuality. Read about: the Sufi poetess Rabia (8th century) and contemporary Sufi master Irina Tweedie; Hildegard of Bingen, Mechtild of Magdeburg, and Hadewijch of Brabant; the Beguines of medieval Europe; author Kathryn Hulme *(The Nun's Story)* who worked with Gurdjieff; German healer and mystic Dina Rees...and many others.

Paper, 35 b&w photos; 520 pages, $19.95   ISBN: 0-934252-79-3

**TO ORDER PLEASE SEE ACCOMPANYING ORDER FORM
OR CALL 1-800-381-2700 TO PLACE YOUR ORDER NOW.**

RETAIL ORDER FORM FOR HOHM PRESS BOOKS

Name_____ Phone (   ) _____

Street Address or P.O. Box _____

City _____ State _____ Zip Code _____

QTY	TITLE	ITEM PRICE	TOTAL PRICE	
1	FOR LOVE OF THE DARK ONE	$12.00		
2	THE WAY OF POWER	$10.00		
3	THE ONLY GRACE IS LOVING GOD	$5.95		
4	MARROW OF FLAME	$12.00		
5	GRACE AND MERCY IN HER WILD HAIR	$12.00		
6	THE ALCHEMY OF TRANSFORMATION	$14.95		
7	RENDING THE VEIL	$27.95		
8	RUMI: THIEF OF SLEEP	$11.95		
9	IN PRAISE OF RUMI	$8.00		
10	MIRROR OF THE SKY, INCLUDES CD	$24.95		
11	MIRROR OF THE SKY, CD ONLY	$16.95		
12	THE WOMAN AWAKE	$19.95		

SURFACE SHIPPING CHARGES

SUBTOTAL: _____

First book $5.00

SHIPPING: (see below) _____

Each additional item $1.00

TOTAL: _____

SHIP MY ORDER

Surface U.S. Mail—Priority   ☐ UPS (Mail + $2.00)

2nd-Day Air (Mail + $5.00)   ☐ Next-Day Air (Mail + $15.00)

METHOD OF PAYMENT:

Check or M.O.   Payable to Hohm Press, P.O. Box 2501, Prescott, AZ 86302

Call 1-800-381-2700 to place your credit card order

Or call 1-520-717-1779 to fax your credit card order

Information for Visa/MasterCard/American Express order only:

Card #_____ – _____ – _____ – _____   Expiration Date _____

Visit our Website to view our complete catalog: www.hohmpress.com
ORDER NOW! Call 1-800-381-2700 or fax your order to 1-520-717-1779.
(Remember to include your credit card information.)

RENDING THE VEIL:
Literal And Poetic Translations Of Rumi
by Shahram T. Shiva

"For the growing number of Rumi admirers, the appearance of **Rending The Veil** *is an important and unique event, providing, as it does, not only a wealth of new and quite beautiful translations but a real insight into how the translator goes about his work."*

- Philip Glass, composer.

The poetry of the 8th Century Islamic mystic Jalaluddin Rumi has been rightly compared in universal appeal with that of Shakepeare and Dante. A respected scholar of his day, Rumi lost his heart and gained realization of his truest Self at the feet of a wandering beggar, the dervish Shems E-Tabrizi. When Shems was either murdered or mysteriously "disappeared," Rumi's grief was inconsolable. In his anguish, legend has it, he turned and turned (the origin of the famed "whirling dervishes"), ecstatically reciting more than 30,000 verses in praise of the Divine Beloved whom he had glimpsed in the presence of the enigmatic Shems.

In **Rending The Veil**, the uniqueness of Shahram Shiva's approach to the Rumi quatrains is that he offers to English-speaking scholars, poets, and lovers of Rumi, an opportunity to "read" the Persian through a brilliant transliteration. Now one can feel the rhythm and rhyme that Rumi himself used when composing these poems over 700 years ago. Moreover, Mr. Shiva has supplied us with a verbatim translation so that we may have a hand at creating our own poetic versions of Rumi as has been done by Coleman Barks, Robert Bly, and many others. This feature alone makes **Rending The Veil** a special contribution to students of poetry everywhere.

A preface by renowned Islamic literature scholar and translator, Peter Lamborn Wilson (author of The Drunken Universe) is a treatise on the magic and responsibility of the translator's art. This book is a treasure for scholars and poets alike.

Cloth 280 pages, $27.95

ISBN: 0-934252-46-7

TO ORDER PLEASE SEE THE ACCOMPANYING ORDER FORM OR CALL 1-800-381-2700 TO PLACE YOUR ORDER NOW. PLEASE VISIT OUR WEB SITE : www.hohmpress.com

SHAHRAM SHIVA

Born in Mashhad in the province of Khorasan in Iran, Shahram Shiva is known for his unique and passionate incantations of Rumi's poetry. Shiva is a major interpreter and performer of Rumi in the West, who speaks the language of Rumi and who has an unadulterated access to Rumi's original Persian poems. He has translated several hundred of Rumi's poems, which serve as the basis for his celebrated concerts and performances. His translations of Rumi have also been utilized by other current Western Rumi interpreters such as Andrew Harvey and Jonathan Star, and have appeared in educational textbooks and numerous other publications. His works include: *Hush Don't Say Anything to God: Passionate Poems of Rumi* (Jain Publishing, 1999); *Rending the Veil: Literal and Poetic Translations of Rumi* (Hohm Press, 1995) which was a finalist for the Benjamin Franklin Award and *A Garden Beyond Paradise: The Mystical Poetry of Rumi* (Bantam Books, 1992). He is a longtime practitioner of Eastern mystical traditions. He conducts frequent workshops and has devised a new, four-step method in teaching the whirl.